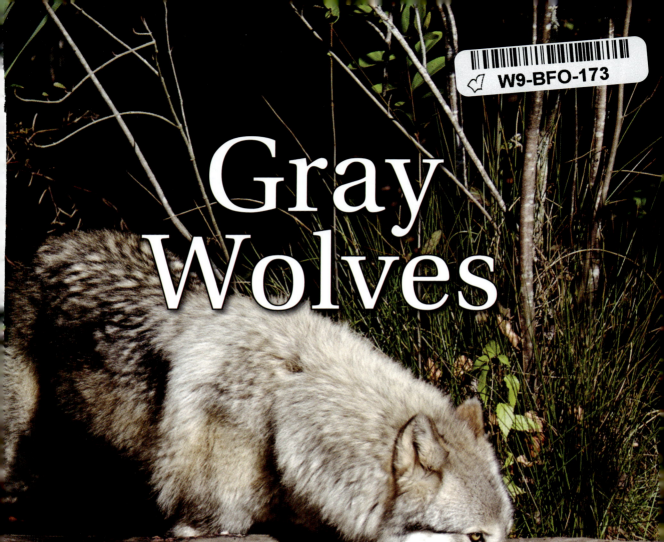

Gray Wolves

Don McLeese

Educational Media

rourkeeducationalmedia.com

www.rourkeeducationalmedia.com

PHOTO CREDITS: Cover: © gkuchera; Title Page: © Korzeniewski; Page 3: © Cybernesco; Page 4: © Tormentor, © Scattoselvagio; Page 5: © Rambleon; Page 6, 8, 9: © Jensklingebiel; Page 9: © Hkuchera, © Outdoorsman, © jimkruger, © silksatsunrise; Page 10: © Freder; Page 11: © F2, © Mrphoto, © Loisik, © Dgareri, © Songbird839, © pac9012; Page 12: © Zebra99, © CDH_Deisgn, © filo; Page 13: © Saipg; Page 14: ©Chrislorenzs, © jimkruger; Page 15: © Jamie Ferrant; Page 16, 17: © Jgrabert; Page 17: © Keramsay, © Outdoorsman; Page 18, 19: © Les Palenik; Page 19: © Rodehi; Page 20, 21: © Moori; Page 22: © Chris Alcock

Editor: Precious McKenzie

Cover and Page design by Teri Intzegian

Library of Congress Cataloging-in-Publication Data

McLeese, Don.
 Gray wolves / Don McLeese.
    p. cm. -- (Eye to eye with endangered species)
 Includes bibliographical references and index.
 ISBN 978-1-61590-271-2 (Hard Cover) (alk. paper)
 ISBN 978-1-61590-511-9 (Soft Cover)
 1. Wolves--Juvenile literature. I. Title.
 QL737.C22M386 2011
 599.773--dc22

                                                  2010009902

Rourke Educational Media
Printed in the United States of America,
North Mankato, Minnesota

rourkeeducationalmedia.com
customerservice@rourkeeducationalmedia.com • PO Box 643328 Vero Beach, Florida 32964

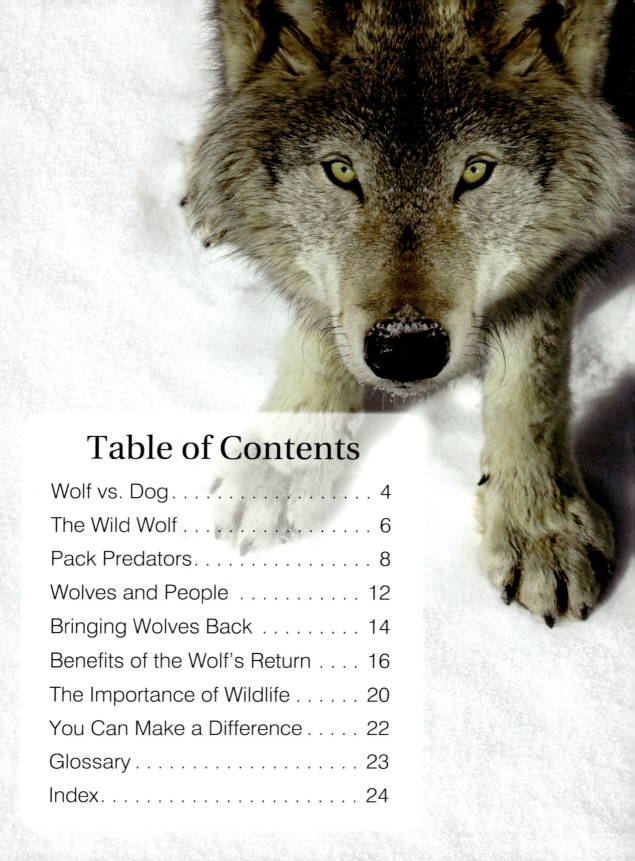

Table of Contents

Wolf vs. Dog. 4

The Wild Wolf 6

Pack Predators. 8

Wolves and People 12

Bringing Wolves Back 14

Benefits of the Wolf's Return 16

The Importance of Wildlife 20

You Can Make a Difference 22

Glossary 23

Index. 24

Chapter 1
Wolf vs. Dog

Does your family have a dog? Then you live with a relative of the North American gray wolf! Wolves and dogs belong to the same family of animals, the Canidae.

Long before there were dogs, there were wolves. Wolves have been around for 300,000 to a million years!

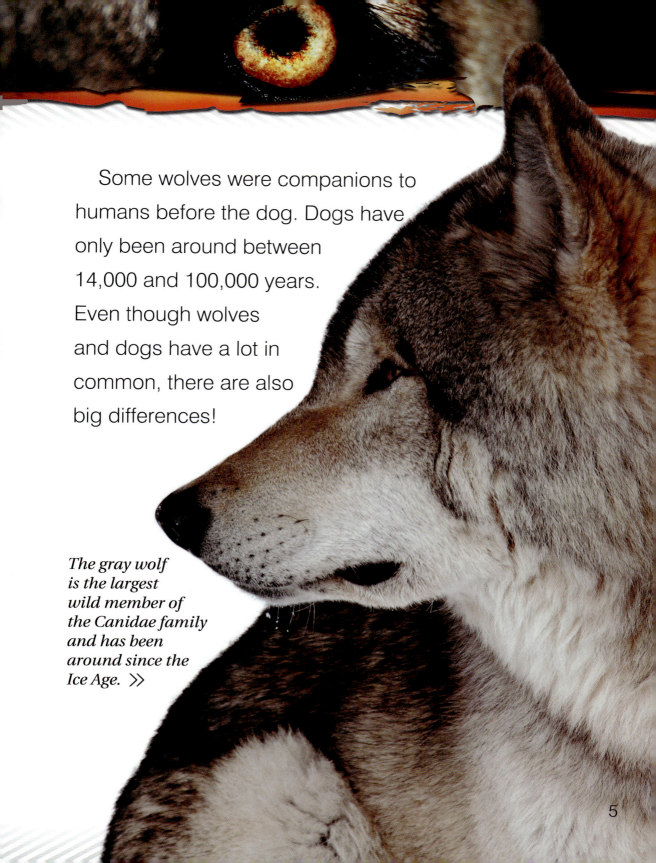

Some wolves were companions to humans before the dog. Dogs have only been around between 14,000 and 100,000 years. Even though wolves and dogs have a lot in common, there are also big differences!

The gray wolf is the largest wild member of the Canidae family and has been around since the Ice Age. ≫

Chapter 2
The Wild Wolf

Dogs have been **domesticated** and are usually friendly. Wolves live in the wild. People consider wolves very dangerous. People often call dogs "man's best friend."

Even fairy tales, such as *The Three Little Pigs* and *Little Red Riding Hood*, teach us about the "big bad wolf." Is the wolf really bad?

When a wolf bares its teeth like this it is a warning that it might attack. »

Wolves communicate with each other by howling, growling, and other vocal sounds. Their howls can be heard as far as 10 miles (16 kilometers). »

DID YOU KNOW?

Wolves and dogs have almost the same kind of teeth. But there's one big difference between the two animals: Wolves never bark. Instead, they howl. A wolf's howl might last as long as 11 seconds!

Chapter 3
Pack Predators

Wolves live and travel together in a pack, or family. A wolf **pack** has five to ten members. The father wolf, or **alpha** wolf, leads the pack. His female mate is the mother wolf of the pack.

Mother and father wolves usually stay together for life and raise their pups, or **offspring**. The pups stay with the pack for a few years before leaving to start a pack of their own.

☆ The adult wolf guards the playful pup.

☆ Here are an alpha male and female gray wolf in the Rocky Mountains.

☆ Pups watch and learn from their parents.

☆ A wolf concentrates and read[s] itself to capture its prey. The wol[f] shares its prey with its pups.

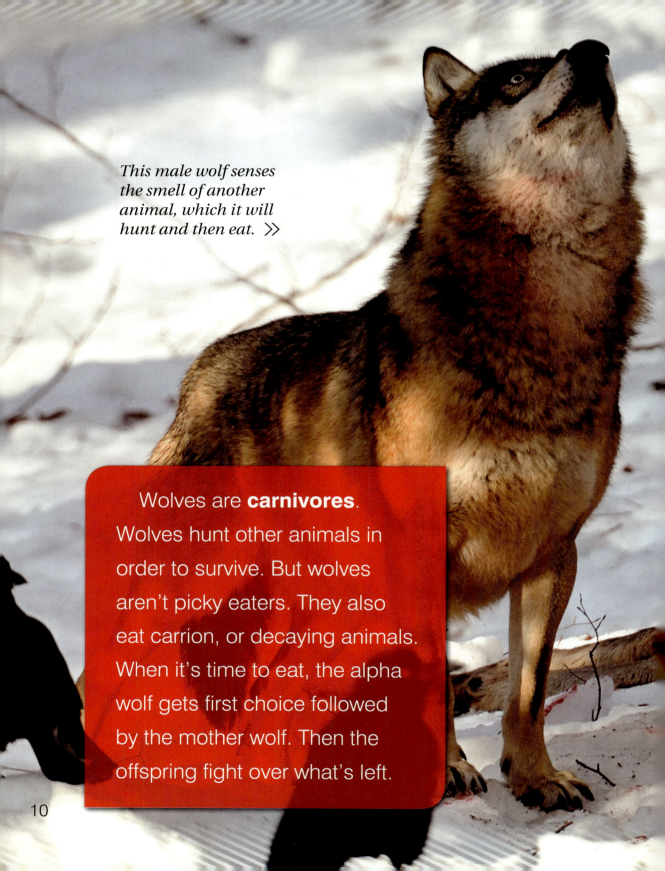

This male wolf senses the smell of another animal, which it will hunt and then eat. »

Wolves are **carnivores**. Wolves hunt other animals in order to survive. But wolves aren't picky eaters. They also eat carrion, or decaying animals. When it's time to eat, the alpha wolf gets first choice followed by the mother wolf. Then the offspring fight over what's left.

Beavers

Rabbits

Mice

Squirrels

Muskrats

Deer

Chapter 4
Wolves and People

Wolves cause fear in humans. But, wolves usually shy away from humans. Wolves cause trouble when they eat farm animals. So humans have killed wolves, making them an **endangered species**. A few thousand wolves remain in the United States. Many of these gray wolves live in northern Minnesota, where there are not many people.

⌄ *Wolves prefer to live in places where there are not many people.*

Minnesota

United States of America

DID YOU KNOW?

Wolf packs usually roam a 100 mile (160 kilometer) territory or an area about the size of Milwaukee, Wisconsin. About 600,000 people live in Milwaukee. The same area would be home to just one wolf pack.

Chapter 5

Bringing Wolves Back

Before the 1930s wolves lived across the entire United States. In the Rocky Mountains and Yellowstone National Park, thousands of wolves lived in the wild. Then hunters killed all of the wolves in the national park. Concerned citizens decided to ask the government to protect wolves in other parts of the country.

Gray Wolves in the United States

MT
ID
WY
MN
WI
MI
AK

Gray Wolf Range
■ Current
■ Historic

Fifty years later, the government created the Endangered Species Act. This act rescued the wolves from extinction. Hunters were not allowed to kill wolves and wolves slowly returned to the wilderness.

Chapter 6

Benefits of the Wolf's Return

By 2007, Yellowstone National Park had 11 packs of wolves with more than 400 wolves in the park and the surrounding areas. The area where there were once no wolves has become one of the best places in the country to see wolves in their natural **habitat**.

⌃ *Wolves keep watch over their territorty.*

⌃ *The wolf pack plays together.*

DID YOU KNOW?

The size of the wolf pack at Yellowstone's Druid Peak varies widely. The pack originally had five wolves in 1995, then 37 in 2002, but only one lone wolf in 2009.

The return of the wolf scared away many **elk**, an animal that chewed on trees such as aspen and willow. Now there are more trees in the park which beavers use to build **dams**. Birds have returned to the park as well.

《 *Wolves are alert, observant, and swift.*

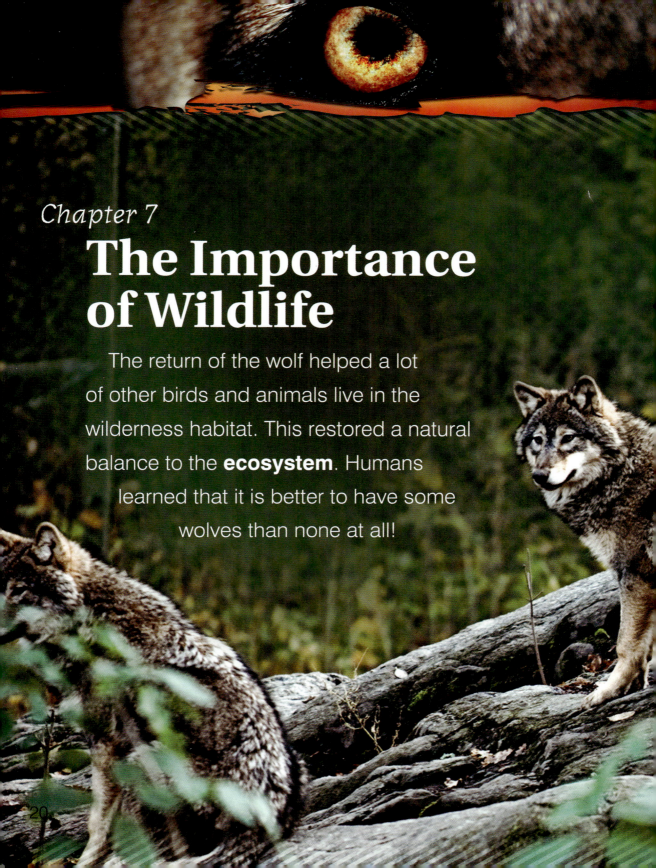

Chapter 7

The Importance of Wildlife

The return of the wolf helped a lot of other birds and animals live in the wilderness habitat. This restored a natural balance to the **ecosystem**. Humans learned that it is better to have some wolves than none at all!

The wolf pack keeps watch and will defend themselves if another animal threatens their offspring or their territory. »

Recognizing a Gray Wolf

Height:
26 to 32 inches
.7 to .8 meters

Length:
4.5 to 6.5 feet
1.4 to 2 meters

Weight:
55 to 130 lbs
25 to 59 kilograms

Lifespan:
7 to 8 years in the wild,
but some have lived 10 years or more.

Chapter 8

You Can Make a Difference

To help protect gray wolves you can join organizations such as Defenders of Wildlife (www.defenders.org) and donate money for conservation efforts. You can also adopt a wolf through the organization.

Keep informed and learn all you can about wolves and conservation work.